A DORLING KINDERSLEY BOOK

Project editor Monica Byles
U.S. editor and researcher Mary Ann Lynch
Art editor Peter Radcliffe
Managing art editor Chris Scollen
Managing editor Jane Yorke
Production Neil Palfreyman and Susannah Straughan

Illustration Simone Boni/L.R. Galante
Triceratops **model** Graham High/Centaur Studios
Model photography Dave King
Museum photography Lynton Gardiner
U.K. Consultant Dr. Angela Milner,
The Natural History Museum, London

First American Edition, 1993
10 9 8 7 6 5 4 3 2 1

Published in the United States by
Dorling Kindersley, Inc., 232 Madison Avenue
New York, New York 10016

Copyright © 1993 Dorling Kindersley Limited, London

Reproduced by Colourscan, Singapore
Printed and bound in Italy by Graphicom

Library of Congress
Cataloging-in-Publication Data

Lindsay, William
      Triceratops / William
   Lindsay. — 1st American ed.
         p.   cm.
   At head of title: American Museum of Natural History.
   Includes index.
   Summary: Text and illustrations describe the discovery and
excavation of triceratops fossils and examine what the evidence
suggests about its appearance and behavior.
      ISBN 1-56458-226-4
   1. Triceratops – Juvenile literature.   [1. Triceratops.
2. Dinosaurs.   3. Fossils.   4. Paleontology.]   I. American Museum
of Natural History.   II. Title.   III. Lindsay, William.
QE862.O65L57   1993
567.9'7–dc20   92-54308
                                                            CIP
                                                            AC

AMERICAN MUSEUM OF NATURAL HISTORY

Triceratops

William Lindsay

Consultant Mark Norell

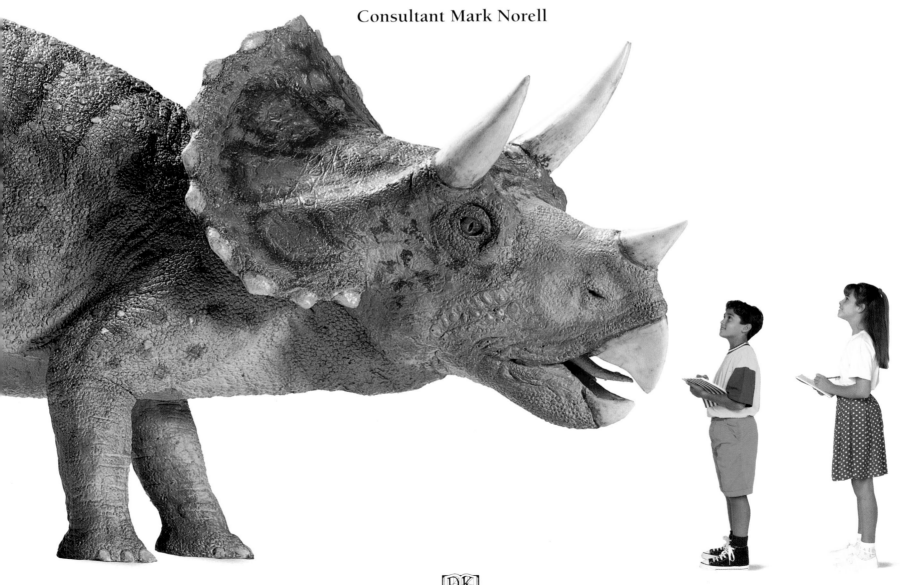

DK

DORLING KINDERSLEY
London • New York • Stuttgart

CONTENTS

LOST WORLDS _____ 8

BURIED TREASURE _____ 10

FOSSIL FRAGMENTS _____ 12

SKULL AND BONES _____ 14

HUNGRY HERDERS _____ 16

HORNED DEFENSE _____ 18

DESERT ADVENTURES _____ 20

DINOSAUR BABIES _____ 22

HEAD-FRILLS AND HORNS ___ 24

TRICERATOPS FACT FILE _____ 26

GLOSSARY _____ 28

INDEX _____ 29

INTRODUCTION

This book is about *Triceratops*, a member of the group
of horned dinosaurs, the ceratopsids, and one of the most
common dinosaurs that scientists have found. Many
different kinds of ceratopsids have been collected in Asia and
North America. By far the most have been found in Late Cretaceous
rocks in western North America. During the Late Cretaceous Period,
this area was at the western edge of a large inland sea. Surprisingly,
many of the same kinds of animals that live today – like crocodiles,
turtles, lizards, and mammals – shared this ancient landscape with
Triceratops and the other large dinosaurs.

Triceratops and its close relatives have a head with a shieldlike frill and
large horns. These horns may have been used for defense from large
meat-eaters like *Tyrannosaurus*. But maybe not. Scientists have proposed
other answers. Some think that the frill acted like elephant's ears to help
the animal cool off. Other theories are that the frill formed a surface
for the attachment of huge jaw muscles, or that the horns and frill
were, like deer antlers, just for show, to scare off predators,
or attract mates.

These kinds of questions are difficult. Even in the case of the
best-known dinosaurs, like *Triceratops*, many questions are hard
to answer, when the only available evidence is the fossil bones.
Understanding the past is not easy, making my job challenging
and interesting.

Mark Norell
Assistant Curator of
Vertebrate Paleontology,
American Museum of Natural History

LOST WORLDS

About 230 million years ago a new kind of animal appeared on Earth. It belonged to the reptile group of animals, like crocodiles, lizards, and birds, but was so different that it came to dominate life on land for more than 165 million years. This new arrival was the dinosaur. Unlike some other reptiles, dinosaurs lived only on land. They had scaly skin and laid eggs, but they also had a new upright way of walking. *Triceratops*, with its huge horns and bony head-frill, was one of the last surviving dinosaurs. Sixty-five million years after its death, scientists are able to find clues about how this dinosaur lived by studying the fossils that it left behind.

Two types of dinosaurs
Dinosaurs can be divided into two groups by the shape and position of their hip, or pelvic, bones. "Bird-hipped," or ornithischian dinosaurs, like *Triceratops*, had the two lower bones of their pelvis pointing backward and down. "Lizard-hipped," or saurischian dinosaurs, had one of the two lower bones pointing forward, and the other pointing backward.

Plateosaurus
"lizard-hipped" dinosaur

Iguanodon
"bird-hipped" dinosaur

Triceratops (try-ser-rah-tops) means "three-horned face."

Triceratops was armed with nose– and eyebrow-horns, and a huge, frilled crest that extended from the back of its skull and doubled the size of its head.

Triceratops weighed over 6 tons (up to 6 tonnes), as much as a fully grown African elephant. Its great bulk was supported by four strong legs.

8

Changing Earth

New kinds of dinosaurs appeared and died out over three periods of the Earth's history. *Triceratops* lived near the end of the Cretaceous Period.

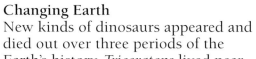

TRIASSIC PERIOD	JURASSIC PERIOD	CRETACEOUS PERIOD
245–208 million years ago	208–145 million years ago	145–65 million years ago

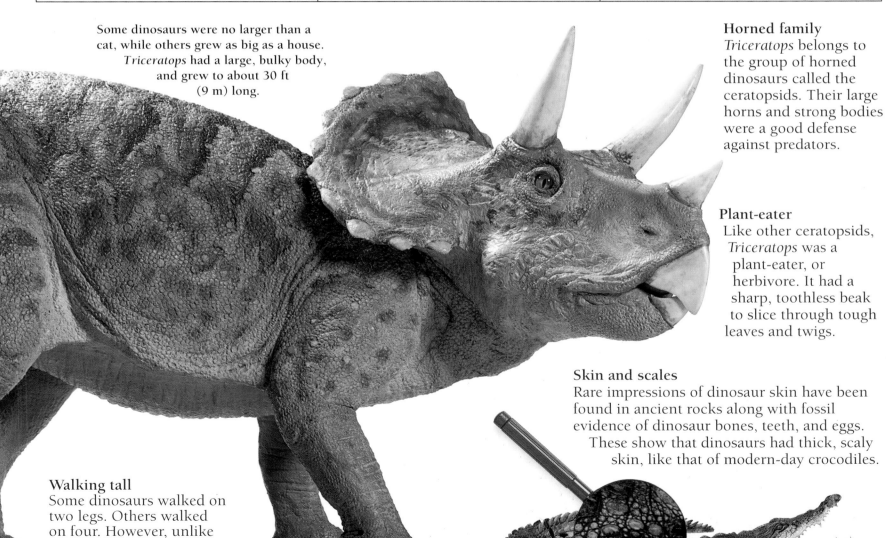

Some dinosaurs were no larger than a cat, while others grew as big as a house. *Triceratops* had a large, bulky body, and grew to about 30 ft (9 m) long.

Horned family

Triceratops belongs to the group of horned dinosaurs called the ceratopsids. Their large horns and strong bodies were a good defense against predators.

Plant-eater

Like other ceratopsids, *Triceratops* was a plant-eater, or herbivore. It had a sharp, toothless beak to slice through tough leaves and twigs.

Skin and scales

Rare impressions of dinosaur skin have been found in ancient rocks along with fossil evidence of dinosaur bones, teeth, and eggs. These show that dinosaurs had thick, scaly skin, like that of modern-day crocodiles.

Walking tall

Some dinosaurs walked on two legs. Others walked on four. However, unlike most reptiles, which have sprawling, outstretched legs, most dinosaurs stood on legs held straight beneath their bodies.

BURIED TREASURE

Only the skull survives of one *Triceratops* that died about 65 million years ago. The rest of the bones may have been eaten by animals or swept away by floods. The skull was buried in the mud and sand of a riverbed, where it was slowly turned into stony fossil.

The skull was discovered in 1909 at Seven Mile Creek, Niobrara County, Wyoming, by the American fossil hunter, George Sternberg, and his family. Parts of another *Triceratops* were found in the same year by Barnum Brown in Hell Creek, Montana.

Fossil world
The *Triceratops* skull found in 1909 is the only part left of this dinosaur that lived about 65 million years ago. The skull was slowly turned as hard as stone by chemicals in the rock where it lay buried.

1 Living dinosaur
About 65 million years ago, *Triceratops* sips water from a rushing river. The river flows past prehistoric trees and plants such as monkey puzzles, willows, conifers, palms, and ferns.

2 Bare bones
A few years later, *Triceratops* has died from old age or disease. Its bones have been picked clean by scavengers and now lie on the bank of a dried-up riverbed.

3 Buried skull
Triceratops' skull lies buried in the mud and sand of the riverbed. The rest of the skeleton has been destroyed by animals, plants, and the weather.

DINOSAUR DETECTIVE
George Sternberg (1883 – 1969)

George Sternberg was the eldest of Charles Sternberg's three sons. He was first taken fossil collecting at the age of six and continued to work on fossils for another 66 years. With his father and brothers, George Sternberg discovered some of the most amazing fossil treasures ever found in North America.

1883	*Born in Lawrence, Kansas.*
1908	*Discovered with his brother Levi the first known fossil of a mummified dinosaur, a duckbill named* **Edmontosaurus**.
1909	*Discovered with his father and brothers a fine skull of* **Triceratops**.
1952	*Discovered the fossil of a 14 ft (5 m) long prehistoric fish, containing a fish almost 6 ft (2 m) long that it had eaten before it died.*
1969	*Died at age 86 on October 23 in Hays, Kansas.*
1970	*The fossil collection at Fort Hays State University, Kansas, founded by George Sternberg, was officially designated the Sternberg Museum.*

Friendly fossil hunters
The Sternbergs, on a fossil-collecting expedition, visit their fellow dinosaur hunter Barnum Brown.

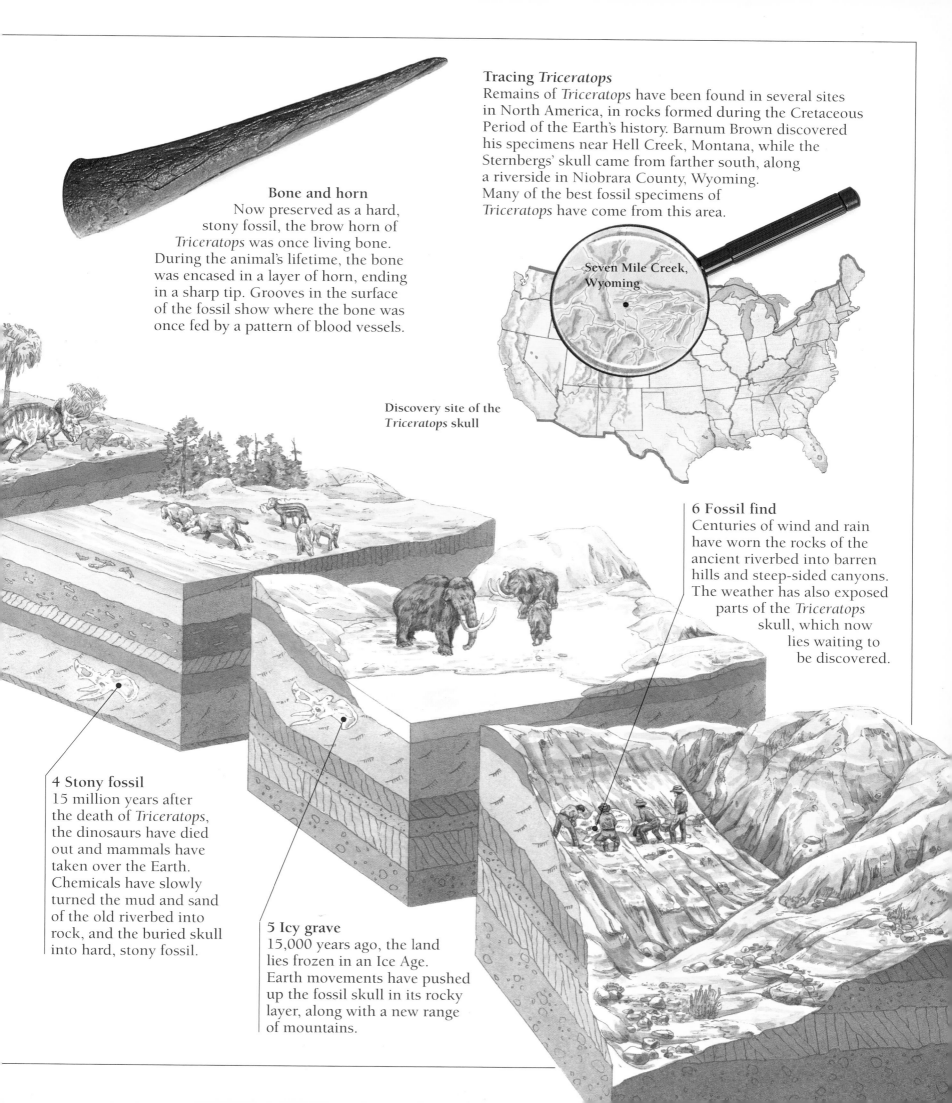

Bone and horn
Now preserved as a hard, stony fossil, the brow horn of *Triceratops* was once living bone. During the animal's lifetime, the bone was encased in a layer of horn, ending in a sharp tip. Grooves in the surface of the fossil show where the bone was once fed by a pattern of blood vessels.

Tracing *Triceratops*
Remains of *Triceratops* have been found in several sites in North America, in rocks formed during the Cretaceous Period of the Earth's history. Barnum Brown discovered his specimens near Hell Creek, Montana, while the Sternbergs' skull came from farther south, along a riverside in Niobrara County, Wyoming. Many of the best fossil specimens of *Triceratops* have come from this area.

Seven Mile Creek, Wyoming

Discovery site of the *Triceratops* skull

6 Fossil find
Centuries of wind and rain have worn the rocks of the ancient riverbed into barren hills and steep-sided canyons. The weather has also exposed parts of the *Triceratops* skull, which now lies waiting to be discovered.

4 Stony fossil
15 million years after the death of *Triceratops*, the dinosaurs have died out and mammals have taken over the Earth. Chemicals have slowly turned the mud and sand of the old riverbed into rock, and the buried skull into hard, stony fossil.

5 Icy grave
15,000 years ago, the land lies frozen in an Ice Age. Earth movements have pushed up the fossil skull in its rocky layer, along with a new range of mountains.

FOSSIL FRAGMENTS

In 1909, the Sternberg family was hunting fossils on behalf of the American Museum of Natural History (AMNH) in New York. The Sternbergs found a fine example of a *Triceratops* skull in the barren hills of Wyoming. They cleared away tons of rock to expose the ancient dinosaur remains.

The fossils were packed up and shipped to New York. At the AMNH, scientists carefully restored the *Triceratops* skull. The skull was then mounted, together with remains from at least four different *Triceratops* animals, to create a freestanding fossil skeleton for display in the Museum's world-famous dinosaur hall.

Charles Sternberg chisels out the skull of a horned dinosaur.

2 Fossil discovery
In 1909, George Sternberg noticed fossil fragments emerging from a steep hillside. He and his brothers began to chip away the stone around the fragile dinosaur bones, using hammers, picks, and chisels.
The Sternbergs slowly uncovered the shattered remains of a *Triceratops* skull.

1 Barren hunting ground
The Sternbergs traveled to Wyoming to hunt fossils in the rugged badlands, where ancient rocks had weathered into flat-topped hills and steep-sided canyons. The dinosaur hunters looked for fragments of fossil, clues to greater treasures buried in the hillsides.

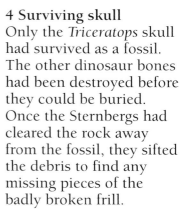

The *Triceratops* skull was found lying upside down.

3 Dinosaur graveyard
One year earlier, the Sternbergs had uncovered fossil remains of another *Triceratops* in the same area as their new find. The sandstone rock layers of Wyoming proved to be a dinosaur graveyard, rich in fossil treasures.

4 Surviving skull
Only the *Triceratops* skull had survived as a fossil. The other dinosaur bones had been destroyed before they could be buried. Once the Sternbergs had cleared the rock away from the fossil, they sifted the debris to find any missing pieces of the badly broken frill.

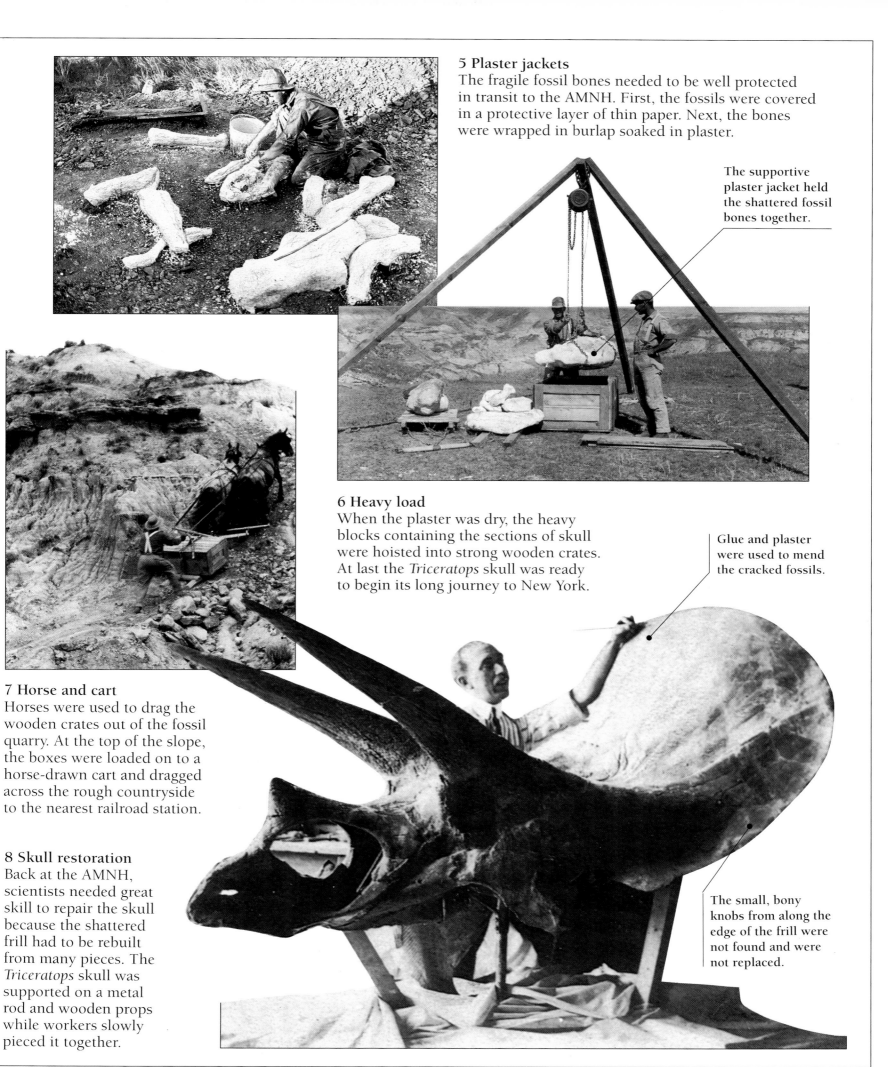

5 Plaster jackets
The fragile fossil bones needed to be well protected in transit to the AMNH. First, the fossils were covered in a protective layer of thin paper. Next, the bones were wrapped in burlap soaked in plaster.

The supportive plaster jacket held the shattered fossil bones together.

6 Heavy load
When the plaster was dry, the heavy blocks containing the sections of skull were hoisted into strong wooden crates. At last the *Triceratops* skull was ready to begin its long journey to New York.

Glue and plaster were used to mend the cracked fossils.

7 Horse and cart
Horses were used to drag the wooden crates out of the fossil quarry. At the top of the slope, the boxes were loaded on to a horse-drawn cart and dragged across the rough countryside to the nearest railroad station.

8 Skull restoration
Back at the AMNH, scientists needed great skill to repair the skull because the shattered frill had to be rebuilt from many pieces. The *Triceratops* skull was supported on a metal rod and wooden props while workers slowly pieced it together.

The small, bony knobs from along the edge of the frill were not found and were not replaced.

SKULL AND BONES

After several years of preparation, the *Triceratops* skull found by the Sternbergs and the skeleton found by Barnum Brown were finally ready for display at the American Museum of Natural History. One of the strongest dinosaurs, *Triceratops*, with its massive horned skull and nearly 21 ft long (over 6.8 m), barrel-like body, was built to withstand attack from the fiercest predator. Some scientists believe that *Triceratops* could have charged at almost 15 mph (more than 25 km/h) in defense against an attacking meat-eater.

Crash protector
The thick skull and strongly built neck and hips of *Triceratops* all helped it to withstand impact when it crashed into an attacker or locked horns with a rival. *Triceratops* could also charge quickly over short distances on its powerful legs. It would not have been easy prey, even for the huge meat-eating dinosaurs such as *Tyrannosaurus rex*.

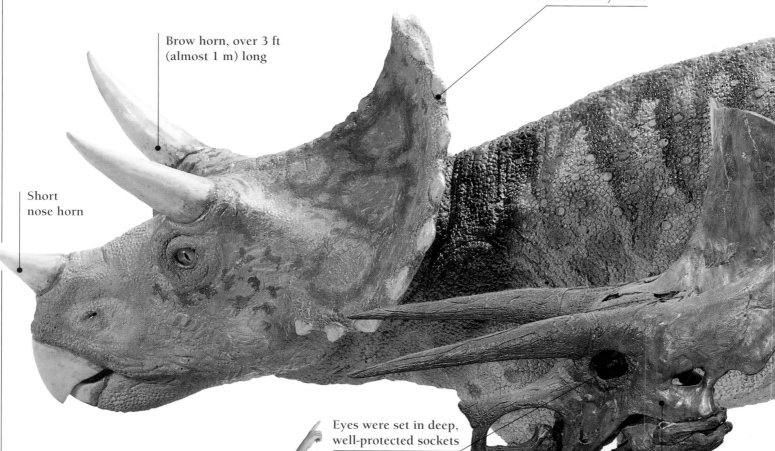

Brow horn, over 3 ft (almost 1 m) long

Skin-covered bony frill edged with a rim of bony studs

Short nose horn

Eyes were set in deep, well-protected sockets

Huge head
The enormous head of *Triceratops* made up almost one-third of its overall length. The head was armed with long, sharp, bone-filled horns on the brow and nose. The head-frill was edged with bony lumps and protected the dinosaur's powerful neck. The horns would have been longer in life, before the outer layer decayed.

Powerful jaws were operated by huge muscles stretching down from the frill.

Humerus (upper armbones)

Row of teeth for grinding food

Ulna and radius (forearm bones)

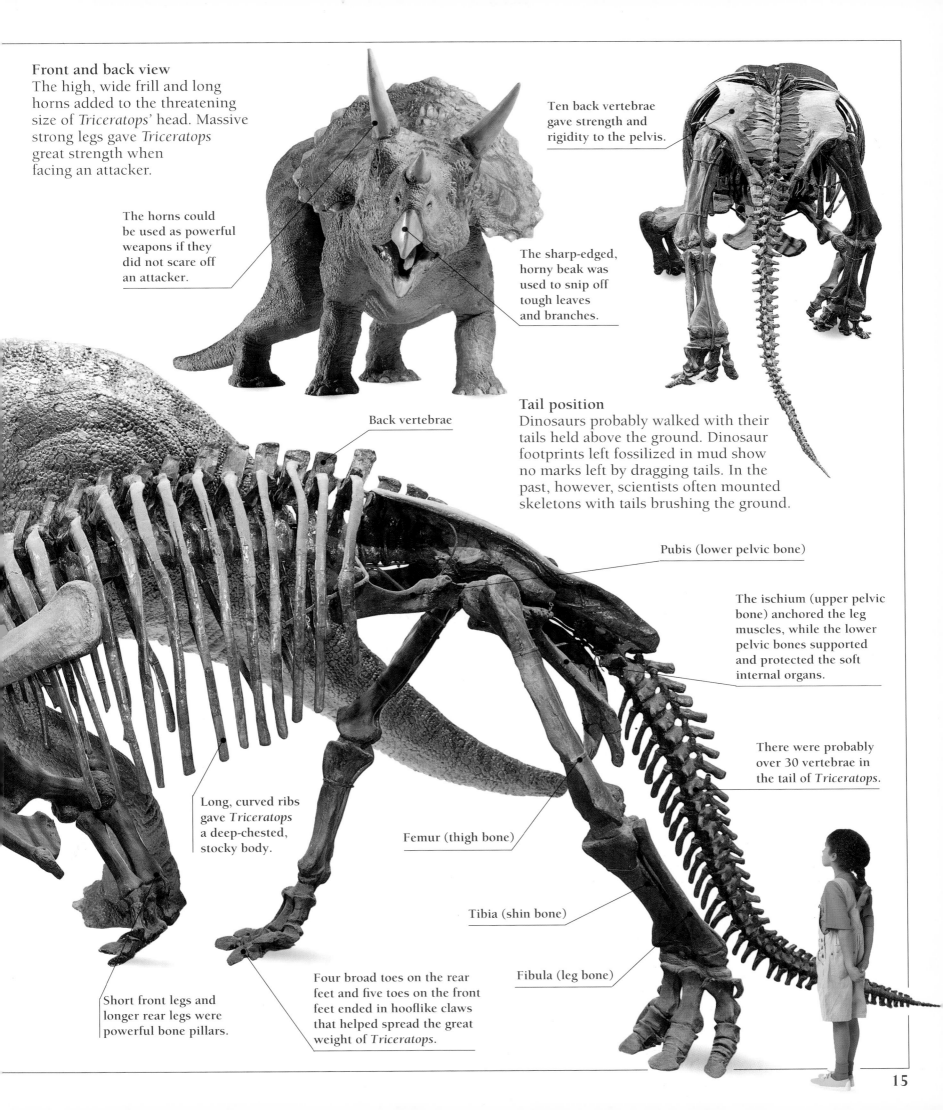

Front and back view
The high, wide frill and long horns added to the threatening size of *Triceratops'* head. Massive strong legs gave *Triceratops* great strength when facing an attacker.

The horns could be used as powerful weapons if they did not scare off an attacker.

Ten back vertebrae gave strength and rigidity to the pelvis.

The sharp-edged, horny beak was used to snip off tough leaves and branches.

Back vertebrae

Tail position
Dinosaurs probably walked with their tails held above the ground. Dinosaur footprints left fossilized in mud show no marks left by dragging tails. In the past, however, scientists often mounted skeletons with tails brushing the ground.

Pubis (lower pelvic bone)

The ischium (upper pelvic bone) anchored the leg muscles, while the lower pelvic bones supported and protected the soft internal organs.

There were probably over 30 vertebrae in the tail of *Triceratops*.

Long, curved ribs gave *Triceratops* a deep-chested, stocky body.

Femur (thigh bone)

Tibia (shin bone)

Short front legs and longer rear legs were powerful bone pillars.

Four broad toes on the rear feet and five toes on the front feet ended in hooflike claws that helped spread the great weight of *Triceratops*.

Fibula (leg bone)

HUNGRY HERDERS

Triceratops was one of the most common dinosaurs living 65 million years ago in the area now known as North America. Huge herds of horned plant-eaters roamed through the forests and along the banks of rivers and the edges of swamps. The hordes of hungry dinosaurs fed on trees, shrubs, and ferns. Only tall plants were safe from the giant appetite of *Triceratops*.

Flowering food
Triceratops and the other plant-eaters of the time ate the new flowering plants, such as magnolia, oak, and laurel, that appeared during the Cretaceous Period.

Snipping beak
Triceratops used its sharp beak to snip off leaves and twigs that grew up to 9 ft (3 m) from the ground.

Growing beak
Triceratops' beak was worn down by its rough diet but may have continued to grow throughout the dinosaur's lifetime, like human fingernails.

Herbivores and hunters
Many dinosaurs fed on the plants that grew on the lush plains. Fierce meat-eaters followed the herds, hunting young or sickly herbivores.

Edmontosaurus
The duck-billed dinosaur *Edmontosaurus* lived in a herd. It could reach leaves on tree branches that were out of *Triceratops*' reach.

Pachycephalosaurus
Pachycephalosaurus had a thick, domed head, ringed by bony spikes, that gave no protection against a predator.

Tyrannosaurus and Ornithomimus
Triceratops had dangerously sharp horns to defend itself against fierce *Tyrannosaurus*. *Ornithomimus* was built like a modern-day ostrich and could have run away from any danger.

Triceratops

Tyrannosaurus

Ornithomimus

Torosaurus
Torosaurus had a huge, horned skull. It was always on the lookout for danger from an attacking predator.

Migration
Triceratops could only survive if it found enough to eat. During a drought, *Triceratops* and the other plant-eaters may have migrated long distances in search of new feeding grounds.

Jaws like shears
Triceratops' tooth-lined jaws worked like garden shears to slice up plants. The flat surface on the teeth worked like a grindstone.

HORNED DEFENSE

Triceratops was well protected against the fierce predators, such as *Tyrannosaurus*, that tracked the herds of plant-eaters across the great plain. *Triceratops* had long, sharp horns on its forehead and snout and specially strengthened bones in its neck, hip area, and skull to withstand shock if it charged into an attacker. If it were lucky, *Triceratops* would not have to fight at all. The giant bony frill that made its head look so huge might scare off any prowling carnivore, or meat-eater.

Attacking monster
A hungry *Tyrannosaurus* spots a *Triceratops* feeding away from its herd. The meat-eater rushes at its prey, hoping to knock it down. It will try to wound *Triceratops* with one fatal bite of its saber-toothed jaws.

Fighting back
Triceratops shakes its head, bellows, and lunges toward its attacker. Charging forward, *Triceratops* tries to stab the belly of its mighty opponent with its horns. If it succeeds, *Triceratops* may escape from death – this time.

Standing its ground
Triceratops paws the ground and hisses at *Tyrannosaurus*, looking for a way to escape the terrible hunter's razor-sharp, slashing teeth. But *Tyrannosaurus* is growing tired and may decide to give up and hunt a weaker animal.

On the move
Standing, walking, or running, *Triceratops* supported its heavy 6-ton (6-tonne) body on strong, stocky legs. The dinosaur may have been capable of short bursts of speed at more than 15 mph (25 km/h).

3 Hip bones take the strain of *Triceratops'* heavy body weight.

1 As *Triceratops* rises from the ground, its long back legs push the hips upward.

2 Huge muscles support *Triceratops'* great body over the front and rear legs.

6 *Triceratops* breaks into a run, perhaps as fast as over 15 mph (25 km/h).

4 *Triceratops* may have walked at speeds of over 6 mph (around 10 km/h).

5 *Triceratops* catches sight of an attacker and prepares to charge.

The rear legs are braced, ready for the impact with *Tyrannosaurus*.

The legs kick up a cloud of dust to try to confuse the attacker.

Means of defense
Triceratops may look a little like a rhinoceros, but it was twice the size and a reptile, not a mammal. Nevertheless, the dinosaur may have defended itself in ways similar to those of a rhino. Some rhinos charge, while others stand in a defensive circle, horns pointing out toward the attacker.

DESERT ADVENTURES

In 1922, scientists from the American Museum of Natural History (AMNH) first traveled to the Gobi Desert in Mongolia in Central Asia. The expedition had set out to find fossil evidence of early humans. Instead, it made the most important discovery ever about dinosaurs. In 1923, the team collected the first known dinosaur eggs and nest, together with fossil bones of *Protoceratops*, the horned dinosaur that may have laid the eggs. Sixty years later, other scientists from the AMNH returned to the Gobi to find out more about dinosaurs and their young.

Making maps
The team's geologist, Frederick K. Morris, drew up detailed maps. These were used to understand the history of the rocks in which the dinosaur fossils were found and to help the team to find their way across the desert.

Site of discovery of the dinosaur eggs, nest, and *Protoceratops* bones

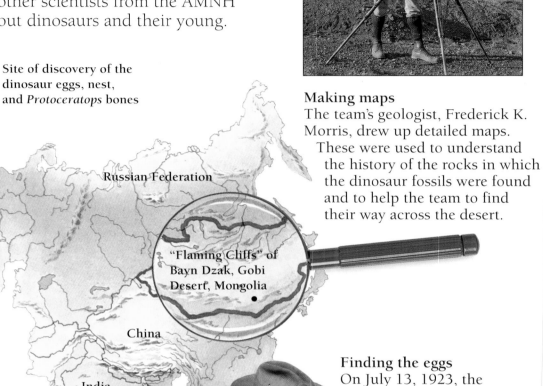

Russian Federation

"Flaming Cliffs" of Bayn Dzak, Gobi Desert, Mongolia

China

India

Dinosaur hunter
Walter Granger was deputy leader on the AMNH expeditions to the Gobi, as well as the chief paleontologist. Granger is seen here, delicately brushing sand and grit from a fossil.

Expedition leader
Roy Chapman Andrews was the leader of the 1923 expedition. He had begun raising funds and planning the expedition several years earlier.

Finding the eggs
On July 13, 1923, the assistant, George Olsen, came across three shattered fossil eggs and some dinosaur bones. Andrews and Granger realized that the team had discovered the first real proof that dinosaurs hatched from eggs, like other reptiles.

Cars and camels
Mongolian and Chinese scientists joined the American team on their five expeditions to the Gobi Desert in the 1920s. They traveled in large cars and met camel trains regularly to receive fresh supplies of food and gas.

Asian cousin of *Triceratops*

Protoceratops was only 3 ft to over 8 ft long (1 m to 2.5 m), about the size of a small horse. *Protoceratops* lived about 85 million years ago, on the continent now called Asia. Its relatives, the horned dinosaurs, such as *Triceratops*, have mainly been found in North America.

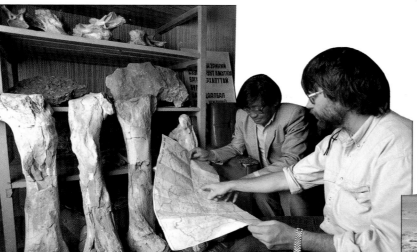

Protoceratops had a beak, short frill, and wide cheekbones. It had no horns, even though it was a member of the family of horned dinosaurs.

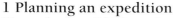

1 Planning an expedition

Since the late 1980s, scientists from the AMNH have returned several times to the Gobi Desert. Before each trip, they check weather patterns and plan routes and exploration sites with Mongolian colleagues, to allow as much time as possible for collecting fossils.

2 Searching for clues

The field leader, Mark Norell, studies debris on the dry desert floor. Fossils look shinier than the red sand and mudstone. Norell studies the fossils to decide whether it would be worth spending time searching for dinosaur remains in this area.

3 Collecting samples

A scientist collects samples of dinosaur bone from the crumbling, rocky cliffs. During the day, the desert is baking hot. At night, it can be freezing cold. Few plants grow here, and any rocks and bones exposed to the heat and cold are soon worn into dust.

4 Excavating fossils

The scientists work slowly to brush away the sand from around a dinosaur skull. They chip away any hard lumps of rock with small picks. The exposed fossil is then strengthened with a coating of glue.

5 Packing up the fossils

Once the glue is dry, each fossil is wrapped in a thin lining of paper, followed by burlap soaked in plaster. When the protective plaster layer has set hard, the fossil can be lifted and carried back to camp, ready to be shipped back for study at the AMNH.

DINOSAUR BABIES

Since the discovery of fossil dinosaur eggs, nests, and bones in the Gobi Desert in 1923, similar finds have been made in many parts of the world. Scientists have been able to use these remains to work out how dinosaurs may have developed throughout their lives, and how they tended their young.

The hundreds of *Protoceratops* bones that have been found range from tiny skeletons to fully grown adults. These bones show how *Protoceratops* changed in shape and size as it grew. These findings may also offer clues to the lives of *Triceratops* and other horned dinosaurs, whose own nests and eggs have not yet been found.

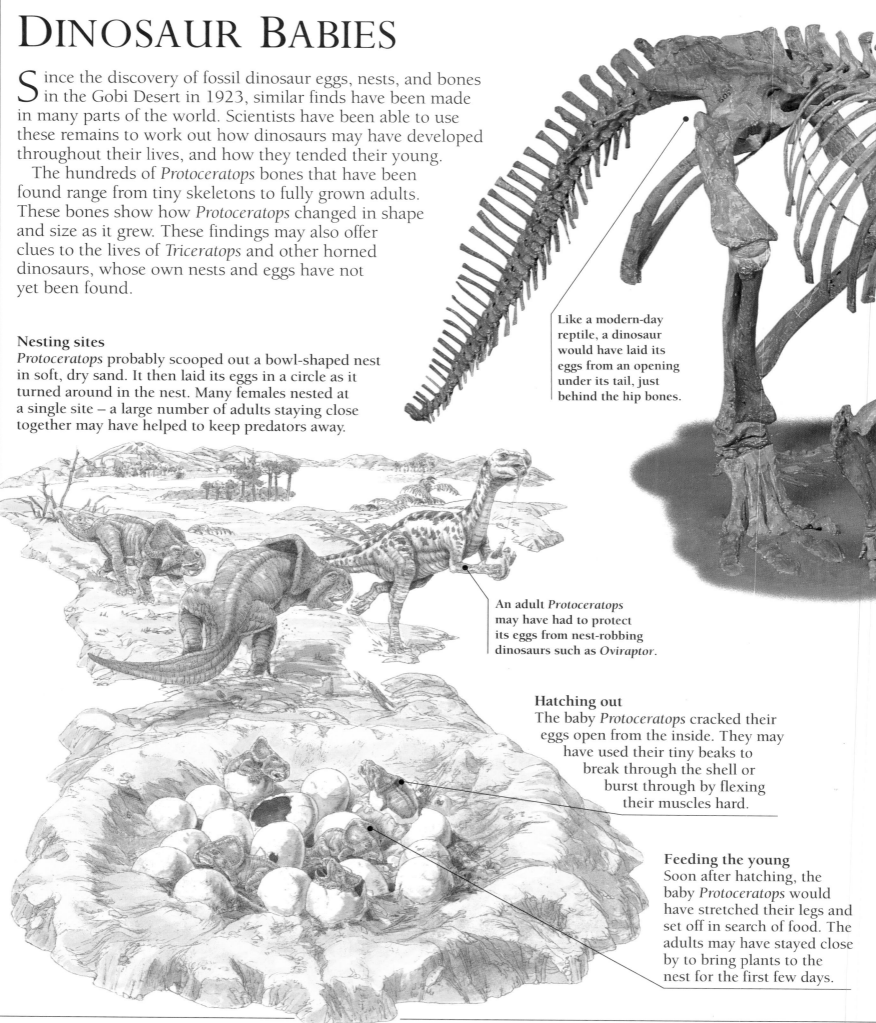

Like a modern-day reptile, a dinosaur would have laid its eggs from an opening under its tail, just behind the hip bones.

Nesting sites
Protoceratops probably scooped out a bowl-shaped nest in soft, dry sand. It then laid its eggs in a circle as it turned around in the nest. Many females nested at a single site – a large number of adults staying close together may have helped to keep predators away.

An adult *Protoceratops* may have had to protect its eggs from nest-robbing dinosaurs such as *Oviraptor*.

Hatching out
The baby *Protoceratops* cracked their eggs open from the inside. They may have used their tiny beaks to break through the shell or burst through by flexing their muscles hard.

Feeding the young
Soon after hatching, the baby *Protoceratops* would have stretched their legs and set off in search of food. The adults may have stayed close by to bring plants to the nest for the first few days.

Short frill

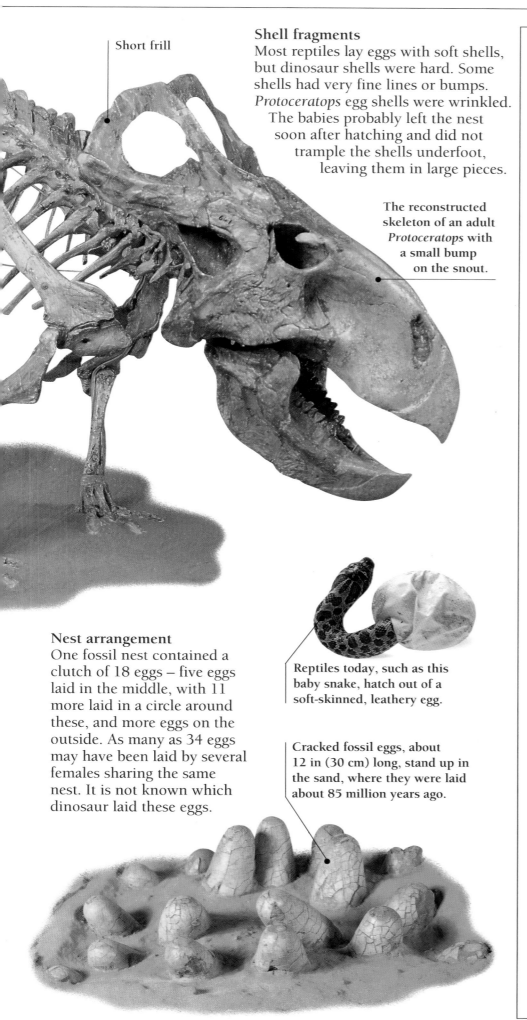

Shell fragments

Most reptiles lay eggs with soft shells, but dinosaur shells were hard. Some shells had very fine lines or bumps. *Protoceratops* egg shells were wrinkled. The babies probably left the nest soon after hatching and did not trample the shells underfoot, leaving them in large pieces.

The reconstructed skeleton of an adult *Protoceratops* with a small bump on the snout.

Nest arrangement

One fossil nest contained a clutch of 18 eggs – five eggs laid in the middle, with 11 more laid in a circle around these, and more eggs on the outside. As many as 34 eggs may have been laid by several females sharing the same nest. It is not known which dinosaur laid these eggs.

Reptiles today, such as this baby snake, hatch out of a soft-skinned, leathery egg.

Cracked fossil eggs, about 12 in (30 cm) long, stand up in the sand, where they were laid about 85 million years ago.

Growing up

Many *Protoceratops* skulls have been found. These show how the dinosaurs' skulls and jaws developed at different stages in growth, from hatching to adulthood.

The skull of a newly hatched *Protoceratops*.

A *Protoceratops* baby has large eye sockets set in a small skull.

The young *Protoceratops* starts to develop more of the features of an adult's skull.

As *Protoceratops* grows older, its frill becomes larger and wider.

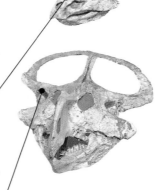

Male and female *Protoceratops* may have developed different characteristics. This may be a male, with a wide frill and a smooth snout.

The growing frill anchors *Protoceratops*' large jaw muscles. This gives the jaw the strength to slice through tough leaves and stems.

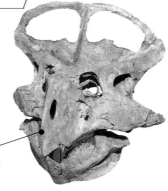

Protoceratops is almost fully grown. Its beak and snout have become narrower, and the back of the skull is wider.

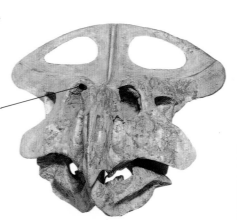

Protoceratops is now a fully developed adult. Its wide cheekbones and frill stand out from the skull.

HEAD-FRILLS AND HORNS

Spikes, lumps, fans, and frills decorated the heads of the family of horned dinosaurs, the ceratopsids. Differences in the shape and size of skulls may have helped the living dinosaurs to recognize one another and indicated whether an animal was male or female, young or old. Head features help scientists to distinguish one horned dinosaur from another, because few well-preserved total skeletons have been found.

In addition to providing armor against an attacking predator, the horns of this dinosaur family probably had another purpose. Just as deer lock antlers today, the ceratopsid dinosaurs may have used their horns against rivals to win territory or a mate.

Some scientists believe that the head-frills and spikes of the living dinosaurs may have been highly colored as a warning to predators or to attract a mate, but no fossil evidence survives to support this theory.

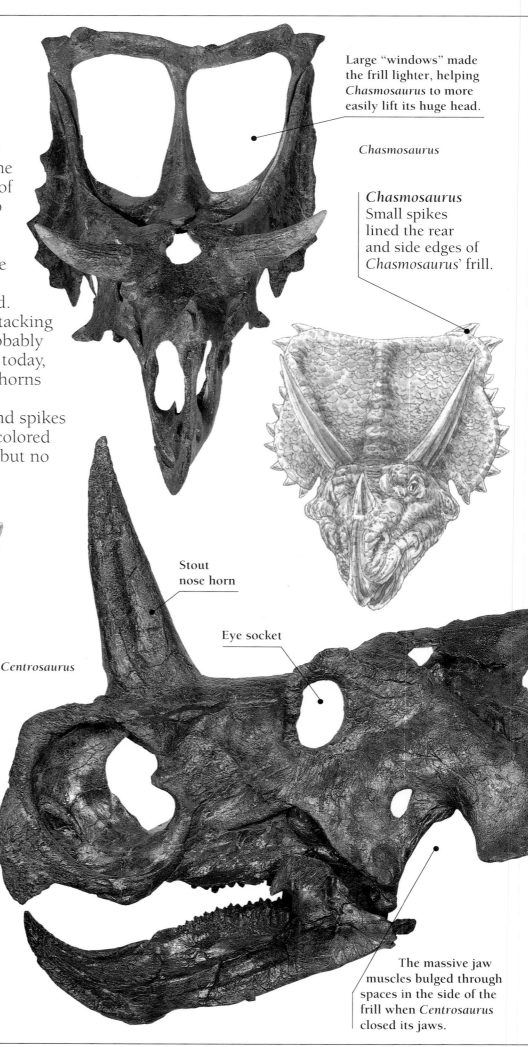

Large "windows" made the frill lighter, helping *Chasmosaurus* to more easily lift its huge head.

Chasmosaurus

Chasmosaurus
Small spikes lined the rear and side edges of *Chasmosaurus'* frill.

Short frill

Sharp, toothless beak

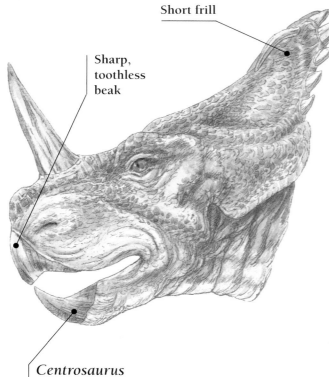

Centrosaurus

Centrosaurus
Centrosaurus had a short frill, but only one horn, which grew high up over its nostrils. A curved spike pointed down and forward above each opening in the frill.

Stout nose horn

Eye socket

The massive jaw muscles bulged through spaces in the side of the frill when *Centrosaurus* closed its jaws.

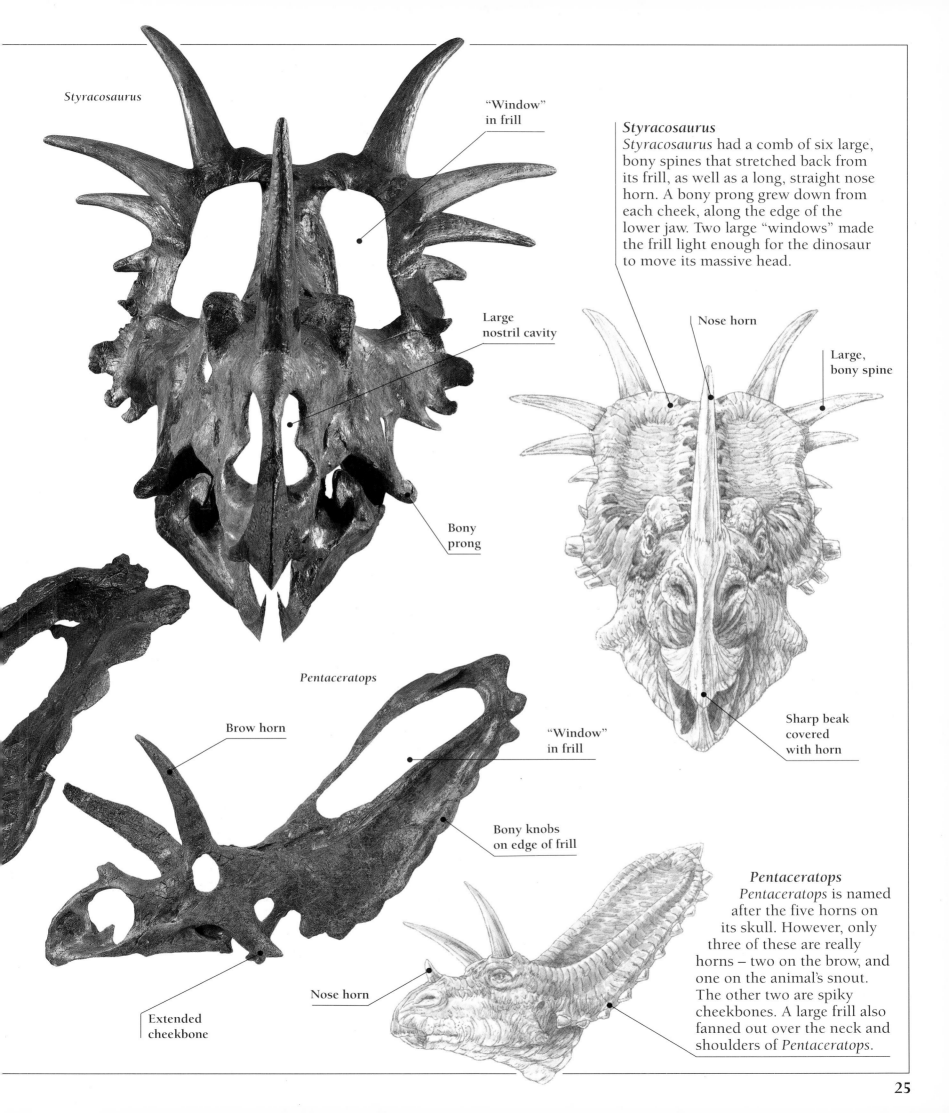

Styracosaurus

"Window" in frill

Large nostril cavity

Bony prong

Styracosaurus

Styracosaurus had a comb of six large, bony spines that stretched back from its frill, as well as a long, straight nose horn. A bony prong grew down from each cheek, along the edge of the lower jaw. Two large "windows" made the frill light enough for the dinosaur to move its massive head.

Nose horn

Large, bony spine

Sharp beak covered with horn

Pentaceratops

Brow horn

"Window" in frill

Bony knobs on edge of frill

Nose horn

Extended cheekbone

Pentaceratops

Pentaceratops is named after the five horns on its skull. However, only three of these are really horns – two on the brow, and one on the animal's snout. The other two are spiky cheekbones. A large frill also fanned out over the neck and shoulders of *Pentaceratops*.

TRICERATOPS FACT FILE

- **Specimen numbers:** AMNH 5116, 5033, 5039, 5045
- **Excavated by:** The Sternberg family; Barnum Brown
- **Excavation:** Seven Mile Creek, Niobrara County, Wyoming; Hell Creek, Montana
- **Bones found:** Skull and most of the skeleton, except for the front limbs; the composite skeleton is made up of the remains from at least four separate animals
- **Where displayed:** American Museum of Natural History (AMNH), New York
- **Lived:** About 65 million years ago, during the Late Cretaceous Period
- **Family:** Ceratopsids, the horned dinosaurs
- **Dinosaur type:** Bird-hipped (ornithischian)
- **Diet:** Plants
- **Weight:** Over 6 tons (6 tonnes)
- **Height:** Over 9 ft (3 m)
- **Length:** Over 29 ft (up to 9 m)
- **Top speed:** Perhaps about 15 mph (25 km/h)

ON THE MUSEUM TRAIL

A museum guide to Ceratopsid specimens
A partial listing of both fossils and replica casts of fossils.

CANADA

(*Monoclonius*, *Styracosaurus*, *Triceratops*) National Museum of Natural Sciences, Ottawa, Ontario

(*Chasmosaurus*) Royal Ontario Museum, Toronto, Ontario

(*Centrosaurus*, *Chasmosaurus*, *Triceratops*) Tyrrell Museum of Paleontology, Drumheller, Alberta

UNITED KINGDOM

(*Centrosaurus*, *Protoceratops*, *Triceratops*) The Natural History Museum, London

U.S.

(*Protoceratops*) Carnegie Museum of Natural History, Pittsburgh, Pennsylvania

(*Centrosaurus*, *Triceratops*) National Museum of Natural History, Smithsonian Institution, Washington, D.C.

(*Centrosaurus*, *Torosaurus*) Peabody Museum of Natural History, Yale University, New Haven, Connecticut

(*Triceratops*) Pratt Museum (Amherst College), Amherst, Massachusetts

(*Triceratops*) The Science Museum of Minnesota, St. Paul, Minnesota

(*Triceratops*) University of Nebraska State Museum, Lincoln, Nebraska

Ceratopsid specimens may also be found in museums in **China, France, Germany, Japan, Mongolia, Poland, Russia, Spain, and Sweden.**

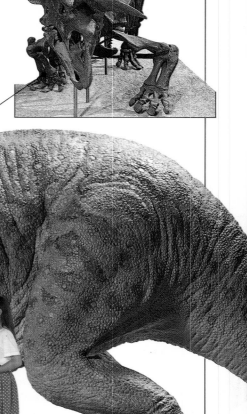

The *Triceratops* skeleton on display at the AMNH was made up from the fossil remains of at least four different animals.

Triceratops was one of the last dinosaurs on Earth. Its huge horns and giant frill made this large dinosaur look even bigger.

Changing world

Dinosaur remains have been found in many parts of the world. New kinds of dinosaurs appeared and others died out as the Earth's landscape and climate slowly changed. This map shows the continents where fossil remains of *Triceratops* and other horned dinosaurs have been found.

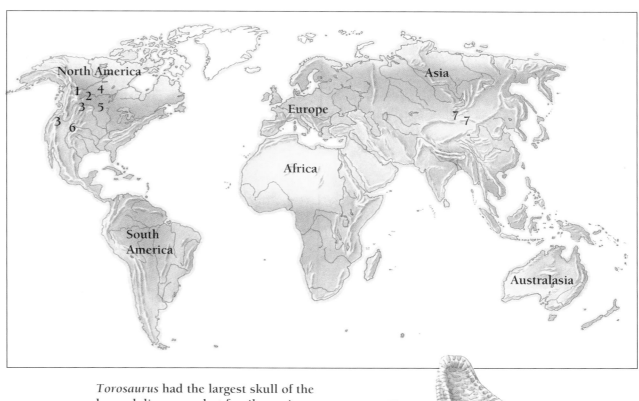

Key to map

1 *Chasmosaurus*
2 *Centrosaurus*
3 *Pentaceratops*
4 *Styracosaurus*
5 *Torosaurus*
6 *Triceratops*
7 *Protoceratops*

The horned dinosaur family

Triceratops was a member of the Chasmosaurines, one of two groups of horned dinosaurs, the Ceratopsids. The Centrosaurines had shorter head-frills and longer nose horns.

A long-frilled horned dinosaur, *Pentaceratops* was about the same size as *Triceratops*. It became extinct just before *Triceratops* appeared.

Torosaurus had the largest skull of the horned dinosaurs, but fossil remains of its limbs and body have not yet been found. *Torosaurus* also lived in the Cretaceous Period and in the same part of the world as *Triceratops*.

Chasmosaurus lived about 75 million years ago. Its fossil remains have been found in Alberta, Canada, and Texas.

Centrosaurus was over 18 ft (5 m) long and lived 75 million years ago in the land that is now known as North America.

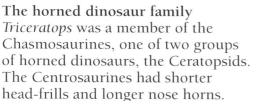

Styracosaurus had long horns and a short frill. It lived earlier than *Triceratops* and, like most horned dinosaurs, has been found in North America.

Protoceratops is the only horned dinosaur yet to be found in Central Asia. It was the size of a small horse.

GLOSSARY

carnivore
A meat-eating animal.

Ceratopsids
The name for the group of horned dinosaurs. There were two groups of Ceratopsids: the Chasmosaurines and the Centrosaurines. *Triceratops* was a member of the Chasmosaurines.

composite skeleton
A skeleton made up of parts from more than one incomplete specimen.

Cretaceous Period
Part of the Earth's history, which lasted from 145 million years ago until the dinosaurs died out 65 million years ago. *Triceratops* lived during this period.

dinosaurs
A group of extinct land reptiles that lived on Earth from 230 until 65 million years ago.

excavate
To dig up an object such as a fossil.

extinction
When living things, such as dinosaurs, die out and disappear from the Earth forever.

fossil
Part of a dead plant or animal that has been buried and then slowly turned as hard as stone by chemicals in the rock.

head-frill
The wide rim of bone that fans out from the back of the skull of a horned dinosaur.

herbivore
A plant-eating animal.

horns
Sharp, pointed features that grew on the skulls of horned dinosaurs. They were made of material like that of human fingernails, growing over a bony core.

Jurassic Period
Part of the Earth's history from 208 to 145 million years ago, when large plant-eating dinosaurs were common.

mammal
A kind of animal, such as a human, that gives birth to live young and feeds them with milk.

ornithischian dinosaur
The bird-hipped type of dinosaur with both lower hip bones pointing down and backward. *Triceratops* was an ornithischian dinosaur.

paleontologist
A scientist who studies fossils and life in ancient times.

pelvis
The group of bones where the legs join the backbone of an animal's skeleton.

predator
An animal that hunts and kills other animals for their meat.

reptile
A scaly animal that lays eggs, such as the turtles, snakes, lizards, birds, and crocodiles of today. Dinosaurs were reptiles.

saurischian dinosaur
The lizard-hipped type of dinosaur with one of two lower hip bones pointing down and forward, and the other bone pointing down and backward.

skeleton
The supporting bony frame inside an animal's body.

specimen
One example of a kind of plant or animal, or a part of it.

Triassic Period
Part of the Earth's history, which lasted from 245 to 208 million years ago, during which the dinosaurs first appeared.

vertebrae
Bones that form the backbone of animals.

weathering
When rocks and soil are broken up and washed or blown away by wind, rain, sun, frost, and other features of the weather.

Pronunciation guide to the dinosaur names in this book

- *Centrosaurus* (sen-tro-saw-rus)
- *Chasmosaurus* (kas-mo-saw-rus)
- *Edmontosaurus* (ed-mon-toe-saw-rus)
- *Iguanodon* (ig-wan-oh-don)
- *Montanoceratops* (mon-tan-oh-sera-tops)
- *Ornithomimus* (ornith-oh-meem-us)
- *Oviraptor* (ovi-rap-tor)
- *Pachycephalosaurus* (pakky-seph-ah-low-saw-rus)
- *Pentaceratops* (pen-tah-ser-ah-tops)
- *Plateosaurus* (plat-ay-oh-saw-rus)
- *Protoceratops* (pro-toe-sera-tops)
- *Styracosaurus* (sty-rack-oh-saw-rus)
- *Torosaurus* (toe-row-saw-rus)
- *Triceratops* (try-ser-rah-tops)
- *Tyrannosaurus rex* (tie-ran-oh-saw-rus recks)

INDEX

Andrews, Roy Chapman 20

baby dinosaurs 22–23
beak 9, 15, 16, 23
bird-hipped dinosaurs 8, 26
bones 11, 14, 15, 18
Brown, Barnum 10, 11

Centrosaurines 27
Centrosaurus 24, 26, 27
Ceratopsids 9, 20, 21, 24, 26
Chasmosaurines 27
Chasmosaurus 24, 27
Cretaceous Period 9, 11, 27

defense 14, 15, 18–19
duck-billed dinosaurs 17

Edmontosaurus 10, 17
eggs 8, 20, 21, 22, 23
eyes 14

feeding 16–17

fossilization 10–11
fossils 10, 11, 12–13, 20–21

Gobi Desert, Mongolia 20–21
Granger, Walter 20

head-frill 8, 13, 14, 18, 23, 24–25
height 26
Hell Creek, Montana 10, 11
herds 16, 17
horned dinosaurs 9, 20, 21, 24, 26
horns 8, 11, 14, 15, 18, 24–25

jaws 14, 16, 23
Jurassic Period 9

legs 9, 15, 19
length 26
life span 26
lizard-hipped dinosaurs 8

meat-eaters 14, 17, 18
migration 17
Montanoceratops 26
Morris, Frederick K. 20

neck 14
nest 20, 22, 23
Norell, Mark 21

Olsen, George 20
ornithischian dinosaurs 8, 26
Ornithomimus 17
Oviraptor 22

Pachycephalosaurus 17
Pentaceratops 25, 26, 27
plant-eaters 9, 16, 17

plants 16
Protoceratops 20–23, 26, 27

reptiles 8

saurischian dinosaurs 8
Seven Mile Creek, Niobrara
    Wyoming 10, 11, 12
skeleton 12, 26
skin 8, 9
skull 12, 13, 14, 23
speed 14, 19, 26
Sternberg family 10, 12, 26
Styracosaurus 25, 26, 27

tail 15
teeth 14, 16
Torosaurus 17, 27
Triassic Period 9
Tyrannosaurus rex 14,
    17, 18

vertebrae 15

weight 8, 26

ACKNOWLEDGMENTS

Picture credits
t=top b=bottom m=middle l=left r=right
Courtesy Department of Library Services,
American Museum of Natural History: Neg.
no. 18541, 10b; Neg. no. 18375, 12tl; Neg. no.
253875, 20tr; Neg. no. 251518, 20ml, 29ml;
Neg. no. 411955, 20bl; Neg. no. 410764, 20br;
AMNH/Fred Conrad: 20, 29tr. Sternberg files,
M. Walker Collection; University Archives/
Forsyth Library; Fort Hays State University,
Hays, Kansas: 12ml, 12br, 13tl, 13ml, 13mr,
13br. Permission of the National Museum of
Canada, Ottawa: 12mr. Bruce Coleman/
RIM Campbell: 19br.

Model photography by Dave King: 2–6, 7tl, 7bl,
8b, 9bl, 14–15m, 15tm, 16–17, 18–19, 26b, 28tr,
29br.

Museum photography by Lynton Gardiner: 11tl,
14–15b, 15tr, 22–23t, 23bl, 23r, 24–25, 26mr,
28bl, 29mr.

Additional special photography by Paul Bricknell:
(magnifying glass) 9br, 11tr, 20mr, 29mr; Andy
Crawford: (children) 5br, 14bl, 26b; (model)
7r, 19tr. Jerry Young: 9br, 23m.

Index by Lynn Bresler.

Dorling Kindersley would
like to thank Katherine
Rogers for her help in
researching images from
the Sternberg files at
the Forsyth Library,
Fort Hays
State
University, Hays, Kansas.

Thanks also to Scarlett Lovell,
Charlotte Holton, and Barbara
Mathe of the AMNH; to Fred
Conrad for his Gobi photographs;
and to Perle A. of the Mongolian
Natural History Museum.